W9-AEI-350

Any Body's Song

Other Books by Joseph Langland

Poetry
THE GREEN TOWN (Poets of Today III)
THE WHEEL OF SUMMER
THE SACRIFICE POEMS
POET'S CHOICE (co-editor)
POETRY FROM THE RUSSIAN UNDERGROUND
(co-editor)

Short Fiction
THE SHORT STORY (co-editor)

JOSEPH LANGLAND

Any Body's Song

MIDDLEBURY COLLEGE LIBRARY

DOUBLEDAY & COMPANY, INC.
GARDEN CITY, NEW YORK
1980

ISBN: 0-385-15895-5
Library of Congress Catalog Card Number 79–8968
Copyright © 1965, 1968, 1975, 1978, 1980 by Joseph Langland
All Rights Reserved
Printed in the United States of America
First Edition

"Reincarnation" and "Winter Nights in the Land of the Midnight Sun," originally appeared in *Epoch,* XXVI, 1, Fall 1976, and "Upon Hearing His High Sweet Tenor Again" in *Epoch,* XXIX, 1, Fall 1979. Copyright © 1976, 1979 by *Epoch.* Reprinted by permission of *Epoch.*

The poems "Intimations of the Ordinary Truth" (March 7, 1977) and "Getting Ready to Really Leave" (August 30, 1969) © by *The New Yorker Magazine, Inc.* 1977, 1969 respectively. Reprinted by permission of *The New Yorker.*

"Sacrifice of the Dandelions," reprinted from *The North American Review,* copyright © 1975 by the University of Northern Iowa. Reprinted by permission of *The North American Review.*

"A Stone for a Maker" originally appeared in *The Massachusetts Review,* Winter 1970. "In the Shell of the Ear," "A Love Song," "Windflower Songs," "The Lotus Flower," "Putting Myself Together," "A Dream of Love," "Farm Boys: The Barnyard," "Farm Boys: The Tool Shed" and "Trilliums, Hepaticas and Wood Lilies." "Walden" originally appeared as "How It, So Help Me, Was" in *The Massachusetts Review,* IV, 1, Autumn 1962, and "Norwegian Rivers" in *The Massachusetts Review,* XVI, 3, Summer 1975. Reprinted from *The Massachusetts Review,* © 1962, 1970, 1975, 1977, Massachusetts Review, Inc. Reprinted by permission of *The Massachusetts Review.*

"A Rural Homily upon Urban Decay" originally appeared in *Shenandoah,* XXI, 3, Spring 1970, p. 197. Copyright © 1970 by Washington & Lee University, reprinted from *Shenandoah:* The Washington & Lee University Review, with the permission of the editor.

Some of the other poems in this volume appeared originally in the following publications: "Conversations from Childhood: The Victrola" and "Conversations in Half-Song: At the American Well" (issue of March 1968) and "Singing in Late Summer" (issue of January 1965) in *Poetry;* "Libertyville" in the Amherst *Record;* "Sibelius" and "The Lover, Remorseful, Writes Once Again" in *A Review,* Amherst College; "A Hiroshima Lullaby" in the *Christian Herald;* "Upon the Origin of What Really Matters" in the *Gob Poetry Pamphlets;* "My Own Country" in *Quabbin;* "A Snowfall" (Spring 1978) in *Spectrum;* "Dandelion" and "Down Under Our Days" in Today's Poets, *Chicago Tribune* Sunday Magazine; "With John Mathison in Wyoming" in a volume honoring John Mathison, *The German Sections of "Vanity Fair" and Other Studies,* University of Wyoming, 1975.

"Thinking of Melville at Arrowhead" (under the fuller title "Thinking of Melville in His Thirteenth Land-Locked Year at Arrowhead") and "All the Lovers You Ever Knew" originally appeared in *The Northwest Review,* X, 1, Summer 1968. Copyright © 1968 by *The Northwest Review.* Reprinted by permission of *The Northwest Review.*

CONTENTS

I

IN THE SHELL OF THE EAR

(for Judith)

Your warm skin is an old road under my hands
as mine in yours. If I have wandered
deep in the cave of your ear,
then hear me out in my watery songs
while your fronds of hair
wave like lilies over the traveled sea.

Though body aches, body is lovely still:
music of muscle,
timpani of bone,
reeds and the gut-strung frets of mind.
Wound to a pulse of bellows, the blood
wanders the blue arterials
into the veins of earth.
If the heart, that live volcano,
troubles the soft and lost subcontinents
for love,
let it burst, at last, if it must.

Somewhere an old horn blows, forever new,
by a dark cave filled with numinous passages
that feed, at last, upon this ancient sea.
The blood rises,
it floods the body's shore
and congeals to grains of salt on a bed of sand,
asleep in the ear of Circe, like a shell.

ANY BODY'S SONG

Here's an acorn from my breast;
plant it gladly, let it rest.
Lie down in its broken shade,
body out of sunlight made.
And if any twig or leaf
fall upon your summer grief
let it root upon the mind
while I catch the autumn wind.

If some little chill should kiss
fingers that my lips did miss,
put your warm hand on my heart
where those chilly rumors start.
If we lie here easy now,
cheek to cheek and brow to brow,
let your sweetly troubled eyes
hide and think our body wise.

Come in to my arms and grow
into me before the snow
takes our warmth and all our good,
frozen, to a winter wood.
Be a shadow for the sun;
be a bough across the moon.
Whisper now above the sound
of dry leaves dropping on the ground.

Take me from these new alarms;
be a lute upon my arms.
Tell me, for the body's sake,

song and lute and heart will break.
Though it bring disaster soon,
I would tremble in this tune
till our bodies rise and fade
downward to another shade.

Somewhere in another wind
lives the lady of the spring;
let her come and teach me grace,
brush her lips upon my face.
Memory tells me solitude
tells a riddle to the blood;
let my heart obey, as well,
beat and heartbeat, like a bell.

If, by chance, I touch your hand
somewhere in another land,
if I knock upon your door
somewhere in another world,
let this oak abide us there,
lift its boughs upon the air.
And let your summer shadows run
through me till our time is gone.

INTIMATIONS OF THE ORDINARY TRUTH

(for F. W. T.)

Yes,
we have heard you whispering at the edges of our houses
in Amherst, Massachusetts,
or standing aloof, questioning sleep
and the drowned harps of the sea.
And now in your tides of surrounding shadows
you are still waiting, turning in blurred rings,
engulfing our watery eyes.
You,
with your great and enigmatic brow
flashing by fires and swords and masked sentries
in the stony frieze of the ages,
we have seen you wither away into genies
in the open palms of our friends;
you,
falling the long trajectories of God
into the brass mouths of bugles,
we have tripped your barreled eye
and heard your polished bell.
Once,
you came at dawn through the meadows of Wyoming
to brush your casual lips upon our temples;
and once,
in a gust of wind near Decorah, Iowa,
we heard, or thought we heard,
your great subtle hooves falling away toward evening

when a few stray raindrops
pocked and powdered the dusty roads;
                              and once,
at high noon in the chilled and rocky streams
you lay for a moment in the riffles of brushed water,
but when I reached out with my hand
only a mossy stone came dripping to the sun.
                              And once,
in La Crosse, Wisconsin,
you loafed at a street corner, a dark stranger,
awaiting only a brief nod,
and, once in a blue moon, a swift embrace
before the lights went down upon that inland river
and slept in all its radiant streams
upon the Gulf.

Beyond those waters, beyond these brooks and tides,
beyond the Caribbean,
adrift in other seas,
this old imagination rides its tough and ghostly sail
on the ring of our blue sphere,
as though by holding a small stone in our palm
we began, far off, to understand
the Alhambra or Angkor Wat,
Chartres or the Taj Mahal or the Parthenon.

There, here now, and everywhere,
these misty proclamations on our tongues
riot our days and nights
and fire us all with immediate history.
The wandering stranger at nightfall

follows the street we all went up and down,
stops with his ear to our homely doors
and knocks. And listens.

The heart rocks and glistens on that shore.

And into the shadow and inner shade of ourselves
we fall, we fall, we fall
like prayer;
while, sure as Sunday, in the old forbidden cities
and the greening mud flats under our broken towers,
we hear that faintly echoing bell,
fired in hills of trees and stones,
kissing the common air.

UPON THE ORIGIN
OF WHAT REALLY MATTERS

(*for Julie and Lois*)

    And,
after a long journey,
we rose upon the pure white breast of winter
    (O child, children)
in the fallen dusk of sun
tunneling into the moon.

    There,
in Highland Township meadows,
a pine tree, somber in its head of boughs,
    (blue-green, gold)
drooped crystals from its stems
and called our shadows in.

    Something
familiar in its arms
fragrantly lifted; it whispered to the dark
    (starlight, starbright)
distance of sheds and barns
and ringed that forest field

    with dreams
of strange illuminations.
But whether music, magic, games or stories,
    (forget, forgetting)

or the gnomes of old desires,
we all, it seems, forgot.

   And
plunging through the snow
we came, once more, along those playhouse roads
      (hello, hello)
   upon men, women, and homes,
   and a huge grave of songs.

CONVERSATIONS FROM CHILDHOOD: THE VICTROLA

Lo, Here the Gentle Lark

When Alma Gluck
sang in high soprano,
   Lo,
Here the Gentle Lark,

on the scratched
ten-inch 78 record
to the old Victrola,

that little dog
was always listening
in the old horn.

Flutes sang, she sang—
larks singing together—
and he began.

And though time
goes terribly round
   & round
I am singing, still.

The Dog in the Horn

You dumb bloke,
you think steel needles
   can go
ten records without a mark?

Yeah, we watched
how the grooves got scored,
afraid the mended rota

would lose a cog.
We even tried group whistling
when the thing was gone.

Money went bang,
depression came, dry weather,
no crops. Man!

Yessiree, I'm
looking for the tone
   and sound
of the world's goodwill.

IN 1912, MY FATHER BUYS THE VICTOR RECORD OF "SEXTET FROM LUCIA" FROM HOEGH'S JEWELRY STORE IN A SMALL TOWN IN MINNESOTA

Charley is entering the record and jewelry store now, a dapper forty-one, just married to his elegant Clara, with nine children still to be conceived and carried and born and raised clear into the Depression. He has just come from the bank, smartly dressed in his tight waistcoat and dark striped trousers. As he enters the door, Ove Hoegh glances up with appreciation: a favorite, a good customer, a friend.

Yes, indeed, he has some new records from the operas: Alma Gluck, some more Caruso, Louise Homer, Journet, Amati, even Melba, and a new quartet from *Rigoletto*. But Charley, I want you to hear this! Ove winds the Victrola, shining in polished oak. My father leans lightly against the jeweled counter and stands on his left foot, with his right balanced across it on the tip of its toe; his right elbow is on the counter, his left hand in his pocket. His head turns slightly outward into the room; he tips it ever so slightly down for listening.

Then the seven-dollar twelve-inch seventy-eight with its red-and-gold heart begins to turn. The shining steel needle, with a soft swish, slowly negotiates the black edge into the deep grooves, and the arpeggio chordal plucking in the strings begins. And then the huge horn hidden in the box behind its fine brocade begins softly singing: sol sol SOL, do MI re DO SOL in its vibrant Italian vowels. The little gallery is transfixed. Waves of harmonic melodies float up

and over, interweave, making their exits and entering again
with violins and rapiers and satin gowns. All their songs
gesture in embroidered pantaloons and waxed moustaches;
pale hands sweep over their troubled foreheads; they
implore the air; they brace themselves on their hips,
indignant, wan, robust, judicious, serene, over the carved
table and the velvet and leather chairs.

Oh, my father is a fine man now, there in that royal box
with all that splendid company! His skull is the
philharmonic of them all, jeweled with sound.

And when intermission comes, he will step out on Main
Street and all along down Division, to greet his Clara
Elizabeth with an amulet under his arms to tell her, like a
messenger from on high, that La Scala has finally
come—Sembrich, Caruso, Scotti, Journet, Severina and
Daddi—all the way from Milano to Spring Grove,
Minnesota, and he is bringing them home.

TRILLIUMS, HEPATICAS AND WOOD LILIES UNDER THE TAAKLE BLUFFS

Thinking of your light body half in water
where North Bear Creek and Rocky Spring together
meet in our bottomlands and valleys—
one from those Minnesota farms and town,
one from these Iowa hills—
thinking of that cool water,
your face half smiling from its surfaces,

seeing your brow above the watercress,
your hair against the quartz and granite stones
hung in the banks of green and tawny grass
where the moon fell fifty years ago,
I watch the sun
hang up its golden question to the sky.

I lift my hands to speak; suspended in themselves
they pause and start again,
letting my fingers memorize these riffles,
rising and dripping and falling,
the whole earth one long breath
of rippling substances.
Then the old willow and the great oaks and elms
put on the smallest breezes, their leaves turning
upon a cyclic pendulum of stems
blending over and over.
                       Seven shades of green
splash in a rainbow of wet eyelids
down half a century where those springlike waters
made for the open sea,

as though, once more, a bell
lifted its crystal lips where the two creeks ran together
and rang its silver tongue
around the sky-blue rim of the limestone cliff
while all the woodlands answered, wild with flowers.

SACRIFICE OF THE DANDELIONS

When all their gold blew up in a cloud
and threatened a silver blight on the land,
the entire neighborhood rose in arms
      and took a hand.

From April we labored to do them in,
ripping their tongues from the spongy lawn
and dumping their heads in velvet piles
      by the old trash bin.

In bags and buckets and wheelbarrow loads
we dug them out with knife and tine
and carted them off to the garbage stalls
      to wilt and die.

Though with the mower I trimmed the lawn
to an inch of its life, those flowers grew
flat on the turf till, plant by plant,
      we cut them through.

What pride and virtue, doing them in,
keeping our lawns entirely green,
graced by domestic flowers, sown
      as those had not been.

When the view from the porch was purely our own,
not a yellow head on the verdant sheen,
we gathered praises from houses and barns,
      being godly and clean.

Yet out in the pastures and barley fields
they gleamed in a thousand beds of gold
and after a week rose up in a cloud—
      oh, we all grow old—

and sailed into silvery mats on our lawn
and clung to our pure green grass like a snare
to give us our virtue for another year
      and keep us right there.

A RURAL HOMILY UPON URBAN DECAY

When weeds six feet tall by the granary
dry downward through September
into their old manures
and take the frost too quickly into their hearts,
leaves fall, raggedly grayed,
stalks fray and shed their skins,
and heavy heads tip over in the wind.
Rain strips them further down,
and pigeons from corncribs
chirr and coo in their soft bones
until those high green palaces of youth
can scarcely hold
a clump of fluttering swallows
or a skittering sparrow.

And soon those weeds lie half in dust,
while sun and ice
break out the cottony pulp from webbed stalks
and shred the cotyledonous strings.
Then only the chilled fragility of snow,
building its crystal scaffolding
foot by silent foot,
holds up those monumental stems
half-stricken in the weather.

There in those broken harps
they sound their blurred demotic songs
wherever they cracked and fell.
And under the snow, unseen,
families of hungry fur-coated field mice

burrow over their roots
and let most any stem
lay out their cellar passageways
and frame their busy neighborhoods of snow.

Wherever they go,
time with its huge soft plow
will turn us down and down again
into our expectations.

So come.
This is the old granary,
and these are our summer weeds.
Briefly now, head bowed,
step into the huge green patch
and breathe the moist pollens.
Desire waxes and wanes.
Instinct falls and rises like a weed.
And memory, like a mouse
sniffing its own tunnel,
saves for its small and ultimate city
something to nibble upon:
a recollection.

AN OLD DISCUSSION WITH MYSELF

They say God loves   and Jesus dies
so that man lives.   Or so the tale
came into fame   for good or ill.

If it were ill   that man loves,
then love-and-fame   most surely dies.
Is that the tale   by which he lives?

For if God lives   too largely ill,
what kindly tale   can be said of loves?
It merely dies   in a mere fame.

So let our fame   try, if it lives
while Jesus dies,   to keep from ill
and halo our loves   with another tale.

If we tell that tale   to a life of fame,
perhaps our loves   will fill our lives
with more than ill   before it dies.

Then, if it dies,   we sing a tale
more good than ill,   more true than fame,
and lift our lives   to a realm of loves.

Neither ill nor fame   lives in this tale.
All that loves dies;   all that loves dies.

A LOVE SONG

When the luminous day, descending
way off through the sharp blue dome of noon,
falls from the hard globe of summer
and waits on the humid horizons,

when the late afternoon
lies on the grayed shingles
of the midwestern farmhouses
like hot silver,

when the light angles and washes
over the tops of the broad elms
downward through the boughs
from leaf to leaf
on the rough trunks with its quicksilver hands
and moves brightly over the grass
and buries its warm fingers
everywhere in its roots,

when the soft clouds, tumbling,
gather from a light mist to a deeper gray
and roll in their heavier shades
around the folds of darkness
and lift the feathery rubble of themselves
out of the west in flowing canopies,

when the wind
rises audibly in the ripening grain
and cornfields trail green streamers over the ground,

and when sudden puffs of dust
break from the farmyard roadways
where a few big drops of icy rain
plop down,

and when a dripping mist sweeps in
while the light mutes to half light and the rain,
draped in its rolling beds,
flashes and powers out of the sky
on hat and fencepost, tree and roof,
mumbling its low thunder,
and that swept music
sings over us everywhere,

and when the grass lies green and clean
hugging the thirsty ground
deep down
and suddenly the water cascades
in troughs and wells and rivulets and ditches,

and
when the late light in the clouds
and the low sun in the rain
relinquish evening into the night
and night to the morning
again,

and when the yellow light from the blue sky
floods along the nearby meadow,
and over the eastern hills
its huge warm face
lightly lifts . . .

BALLAD IN A SUMMER SEASON

Over the valley hills
of Iowa
slowly the darkness fills
all of the draws.

Down from the hanging sky
one star or two
falls from the jeweled night
like morning dew.

Summer is gentle now,
daylight a dream;
grass is a kingdom here,
hope is a queen.

Sheep in the bottomland,
cows by the barn,
all of my windows are
open at noon.

If you still love me now,
shed, house and barn,
I am still bold enough
to keep you warm.

Knock at my ready breast,
toll my heart-bell;
all of my valley sleeps
under this hill.

MY OWN COUNTRY

(for Joey, Buffie, and Paul)

    At home in my own country
riding three horses   bareback into the morning,
    jogging out under the early blue
patched skies   with a vague white
    mist in the valleys,

    we hear the breathing
silence. Dew   hangs in tall grasses.
    On the ridge past Bekkan's Barn
sunlight is sifting   gradually through
    oaks and cottonwoods.

    Under our bodies
the trim hooves   of one brown and two
    matched dapple-gray horses clop
and muffle the dust.   Our leather bridle reins
    lie on their lean necks.

    A frightened
speckled grouse,   scattering the quackgrass,
    churns upward into a ragged flock
of chittering sparrows.   A few late chills
    shiver the edge

    of the barley fields.
On the next hill   Thor Flatberg's chimney
    puffs with a wisp of wood-smoke.
We turn and smile,   softly bouncing
    on Jupiter, May and June.

He rears and whinnies,
shaking his sloppy bit;   May snickers and
    chuckles with her blubbery mouth;
June, prancing sideways,   suddenly farts
    and kicks her heels.

We roll and rise
easily and slowly   upon their silken backs.
    Our faces lift to the long light
over the eastern woods;   our sinewy thighs
    are warmly filled

until time stops.
You didn't ask me   but I want to say
    we all, yes, all of us, love
her who rides   beside us, and him
    who rides beside us,

and the great mild beasts
nibbling the sharp air   with tough lips
    through the Folkedahl Meadows,
and grazing our legs   with warm flanks
    and flowing manes.

We laugh. The horses
break into a hard trot   and then float off
    over the brief robes of morning
into a gallop, and   we are three swallows
    among the noisy sparrows.

ORIGINS

And did that sweetness rise
like sap from the ground?
That burr oak shake the skies?
And the taproot sound

its nerve to the clear spring
where the well-waters roll
under the rusted pump?
Was this the cellar hole?

Or these the splintered boards
that made the barn strain
downward again and again
with corn and grain?

If this is a family tree
then let it, shoot by shoot,
put out a forest of leaves:
bough, trunk and root.

II

LOST FACES

Then,
turning the corner of our little town
in southeastern Minnesota,
I came upon your face, aloft in light,
held to a shadowed angle in the sun.

I had never met you before, never in all the world,
but there you were, there in my little town,
as though you had always been
walking there up and down.

Nothing seemed out of place,
your dress, your hair, the color of your eyes,
the contours of your face.
It was so natural, so absolute a grace
that there was no surprise . . .

only, by chance,
some recognition in your glance
that parted my lips to say hello
to someone I had never known.

You seemed, at once, a neighbor to my heart
and made a usual day of wind and sun
with white clouds drifting in the sky
so strangely local that we seemed to step
right from the sidewalk to each other's arms,

although we only paused
a second at that corner there, no more,

and barely touched each other, passing through a door
of shade and sunlight, hinged upon our hands,
took a few troubled steps,
looked backward, but at different times,
and went on to our private lands.

It was as though the quickened heart had sent
a frontier expedition from its breast
across the Mississippi, going west,
and rode the far Dakotas, mound and plain,
two thousand miles of wilderness and rain,
while all the sky
abstracted in its own renown
to one blue eye,
sent back into my life and to my town
only its mute report,

as though eternity had made a stop
somewhere west of the mountains where the mind,
body and heart,
might sit on a sunny headland, gazing out
past rock and wave and mist of what we are and seem
upon the blue Pacific, like a dream.

WINTER NIGHTS IN THE LAND
OF THE MIDNIGHT SUN

*(for Trygve Larsen and Knud Hammervold, upon being
given a home for the night with them in Kautokeino,
North Norway, after traveling with some Laplanders
and a herd of 2,000 reindeer)*

Cloudberries rise from the snow,
and black crows, feather-thin;
    dwarf branches hone
    cold rime in gold;
Reindeer-Lapps run in their skins.
All sway to mountainous viddas in Finnmark and in Troms.

We arrive, far up, unknown,
a friend, perhaps, of a friend,
    and may go, who knows,
    each one to his own,
and each to his polar end,
never, no never, ever, to gather our hands again.

Or maybe, to meet the mind
calling back something it knew
    whenever the wind's
    strange discipline
swings almost true north true
on Alta and Lyngen fjords its long deep thought of you.

Or else, when gratitude,
tried in its loneliest place,
    learns that our blood
    need not be rude

in any such alien place,
endures, and becomes familiar, taught to a different face.

Then every door and street
is like your own home town,
    its hills complete;
    our rivers meet
and flow, together, down
into those great wild seas, conversing underground.

By chance, so might we too
have been merely traveling on
    over longitudes
    and up latitudes
where we just might never have come.
But then we smiled and met, and sat down in your home.

SIBELIUS

It is nine-thirty in the morning. On the phonograph
Colin Davis is leading the Boston Symphony in the Fifth
Symphony of Sibelius when I particularly notice a single
chord. It is one of the many moments in that great Finn
when, after some fairly vigorous explorations in the brass
and woodwind sections, filled in with heavy drumming, it
seems that they are all seeking some harmonious home.
Then something momentarily resolves, and there, yah! the
chord is. Yah! Large, rich, fulfilled, and then held.

The strings shimmer around it; the timpani keep up,
pianissimo, their almost imperceptible vibrato. The sun
floods in the windows. Everyone in the house stops talking.
One can even hear the teakettle humming in the kitchen.
Outside, the snow lies under the winter birches, radiant and
white, and on the porch railing one small icicle gives off, if
you see it just right, a fleeting spectrum of the rainbow. For
maybe all of ten or twenty seconds you simply stand there in
the house, your mouth slightly open, your eyes looking
nowhere, and just do not breathe.

Then Jan, the old Finn, lets out a blast on the
trombone; the horns shout wildly; the woodwinds pick up
the echoes and swirl in high excitement, and the violins in
chorus follow in full pursuit over the next hill. Everybody in
the house starts talking again, all at once.

Yah! Spring is coming!

NORWEGIAN RIVERS

*(for the sesquicentennial of Norwegian
immigration to the United States, 1975)*

Yah, they are so kind of restless,
rushing around hills
and tumbling the polished stones;
they always have somewhere to go.
Even when they pause in precipitous valleys
they climb
into deep long cold lakes
and then again begin
rapidly falling.

Yah, we have seen them
pouring off mountaintops
like the first dream of a second flood.
And now, one hundred blood years later,
they amaze Norwegian-American travelers,
sailing the birdlike ferries
toward the evergreen towns
or running through summer on the cliff-hung roads
with the sheer bravado of their origins.

Yah, now shall they see,
the affluent grandchildren,
how strong and supple minds
ran those rebellious rivers into the sea.
And now, yah, shall they hear
the low music of springs
watering those impoverished mountain meadows.

Then let them guess as they can,
yah,
how the terrible excitements of alienation
fell on the manhood of our great-grandfathers
and the playfulness of their children,
then rose in a heartbreaking cry from their limbs
and washed from their empty hands.

Then, yah, it was then,
stout in their sadness,
they stuffed their childhood into rosemaler trunks,
clamped them with iron bands
locked once and for all on the eastern hemispheres,
and down those rutted trails and noisy rivers,
out through the western fjords,
they rode for half a century over the Atlantic
on one great ascending wave
toward the virgin hills and the wide inland valleys
of Iowa, Minnesota and Wisconsin.

And now, yah, even now,
grandmothers sitting in their rocking chairs
and watching their children's children
in Bergen and Decorah, Hardanger and St. Paul,
say, half to themselves,
yah, they are so kind of restless,
they always have somewhere to go,
hearing under their vaguely troubled
half-drooping eyelids
the melancholy of those hard hills
and those old stones,
and rivers calling under the walled-up fjords
to the muffled horns of the sea.

AT THE AMERICAN WELL

Source	*Mouth*
This is the source:	Yes, of course.
a spring in Minnesota grass	One must say what he has,
in Itasca Park, now.	somehow.
Come, let us sit	No, not all of it.
by the Mississippi. Passion	I imagine a fine discretion
does what it does,	helps sustain us,
ebbs and flows,	even in those
even in old professionals	fashionable confessionals
in their asperity.	dripping with sincerity.
If the eyes hunt	Well, yes, we want
dark thickets, vague fears,	numerous anonymous ears
are they aware	listening everywhere
they are less able	at the next table,
to join the double gloom	in the adjoining room,
of their discrete	following a street,
self and place? Drinking	spying and thinking
these waters of one nation	with instinctive admiration,
one begins to see	reserved and free.
what he is about.	No, not without
There is always history	some ultimate mystery
which is half wise	in their eyes.

with these blue
original springs, white
with clear themes.

What shines
is, yes, free and dear
and, in a way, true.

Though waters spill
on these prodigal grounds
in the Upper Midwest,

they drift
down through soil and rock,
rise and flow south.

All that is true
to the parabola, night,
and its circling dreams

is curved lines;
no end is ever clear
to the long view.

Something in the will
keeps the involute sounds
in a silent West

where they lift
our daily speech and talk
from heart to mouth.

FARM BOYS: THE BARNYARD

A horse's head is a Greek god,
even when hung in a stall in the barn.

A cow's eyes are bleak moons:
nothing for God to land upon.

A chicken's head is a snake's tongue;
yes, envy feathers its own poison.

A ram's prick is a soft lamb,
and the rough wind is the flower's friend.

A lamb's tail is a flick of the eye;
following whims takes too much time.

The rib of a boar is its own bristle,
and the bag of a cow its own kiss.

I love you dirty, I love you clean:
wheelbarrows of shit, barrels of grain.

FARM BOYS: THE TOOL SHED

Old spade, tell me how you love the dirt.
True, I work best when utterly clean.

Rake, I have pulled you through gravel and hay.
Love must level with what it has made.

The head of the axe is blunt and keen;
so are your eyes, cutting me down.

Saw, if I file you down to your teeth
will you feed me a fire fit for my hearth?

A scythe must scythe and a fork fork;
the hammer hammers and the saw saws.

So, hammer, I ask you to hit the nail hard.
How else can a farmer hang on to his farm?

These saws are heavy with a steely grace,
being most ready when kept in their place.

MEADOWLANDS

Walking through meadows on a summer mountain
on any morning anywhere in the world
one can come upon a flower
more blue than any valley lake or stream
as though earth took from its best altitudes
a heavenly tone.

So in a small and rocky field
in Northern Iowa near the Mississippi
a honeysuckle hung its medieval bell,
a castle in the air.
I touched its portals with my tongue
and with the wild wood lilies, hand in hand,
walked through the ragged ferns
to where the clouds went floating, room to room.

So in the Temple Hills by the Pacific
where the beaches of Laguna ride
down from their rocky shores,
when raindrops cool the sun
in February grasses
the yellow poppies shine.
We float above, impossible and huge
in our benumbing space
and see, far off, the world from which we came,
blue waters circling halfway round the globe.

So in the foothills west of Laramie
where Snowy Range rides upward to its name,
the bluets, Indian paintbrush, buttercups,

sweet william, larkspur, in their beds of green
unfold the sharp white light
toward distillations and such cool fragilities
that children float toward us
with music in their hands
and drape those earthen rainbows in our palms.

So in the watershed wilderness
of the Quabbin Singing Grounds
in western Massachusetts, before the sun
breaks on the scrub-grass clearing in the pines,
woodcocks circle and strut,
dancing their hens from moss to tuft,
and fluff their feathers over last year's leaves
while their hot blood
dies toward a breathless landing
over that grassy sea.

Amazed, the morning traveler
takes on that blur of wings and meadow sounds
while the shy heart, confused with love,
floats off and flops among those meadow grounds,
stammering "hello" and murmuring
in its unexpected home.

SONG AT EVENING

Alone, the evening falls on me
along the cloud-swept day;
I walk the dusty roadway with
the soft feet of rain.

If you, beside your lonely bed,
say for me one prayer
I would not care if anyone
knows all my tears.

I stood beside the edge of town
and tried a broken tune;
if you should hear that wayward song
tell me, you'll come.

I saw a flower hanging low
by a still blue pond,
and as the rain and sun came down
it opened. That was all.

NOT QUITE A CONVERSATION

He and Her	*She and Him*
Two. They bow and sigh	When two hearts lie
down to their own	openly to their
conceptions.	affections
On an enormous room	they wrangle like doom.
he raps, crying: how	Who is knocking now?
will her doorman come?	Who's come? No, no,
Does	that was
anyone ever do	someone I never knew.
all that he thought	Oh? Simply passing
he knew?	through.
Or must he believe	What can the keyhole
this dream	or key
fails as the one before?	do for the barred door?
Maybe no one *was* there,	Maybe no one was *there,*
not even *you,* not	*not* even you, not
even you,	even *you,*
not even you.	not *even* you.
Why was anyone	And long before these
born	worn
to trample the crushed	syllables take their
gravels	travels
looking for you?	there's less to do.

No, she couldn't.
  Who?
I mean, if anyone ever
  asks
that silent door,

"Has she gone away?"
what will it say? I mean,
  say!
God, who's to blame

when the very air stands
listening to itself
  in pure,
utterly pure, dismay?

What does the keyhole
say to the key,
  or the strong
door to the iron bar?

Or flocks to the knoll?
Or almost any bird
  to the air?
Or the shore to the sea?

Yes? You did say yes?
  You,
still waiting in white
  masks?
Yes, he understood
  before

but not enough to say,
perhaps it's better
  this way;
that's not why he came.

So he stands in silence
listening to a pure
  silence
and turns away.

What does the key
say to the keyhole,
  or the long
bar to the oaken door?

Or we to the rocks
of loneliness, when
  any word
might be of the sea?

THE LOVER, REMORSEFUL,
WRITES ONCE AGAIN

Only feeling a word sliding across this page,
   I wonder where you went and how you are,
      no longer helpless in a rage
         but helpless, only,
knowing how hard my answer was, how lame.

Feeling only a word sliding across this page,
   wanting to touch you, desire only a bar,
      myself like iron still, I cage
         myself too strongly,
stoned on this cold reward, a crying shame.

Feeling a word only sliding across this page,
   I rip it out, then patch it back, at war
      with mind, friends, or any sage,
         however warmly.
Alone, ill-starred, okay, I take the blame.

Feeling a word sliding only across this page,
   I throw it at you like that wasted star
      flashing to darkness. Our gone age
         was not comely.
Who won? Not us. No one can guard that flame.

Feeling a word sliding across only this page,
   I cry, forget that now. All that I dare
      is hope you'll come back to this stage,

however blindly,
for fun, not unrewarded, as you once came.

Feeling a word sliding across this page only,
I hope you love me still. Wherever you are,
forgive my need, my self, my rage.
It's been an age!
I'm done in, taking it hard, writing your name.
Only you are the word, you and your name only.
Besides, I'm lonely.

ALL THE LOVERS YOU EVER KNEW

Follow in the morning
    over the hill;
follow in the evening
    under every will;
Far under the starlight,
    under the moon,
all the lovers that you ever
    knew come home

One out of the valley,
    one in the town,
one under the sea-cliff
    washing in the foam,
one over the mountain
    under the moon,
all the lovers that you ever
    knew come home.

Who sleeps in the valley,
    who in the town?
Who followed the sea-cliff
    wild into the foam?
Who's lost in the mountain
    under the moon?
All the lovers that you ever
    called your own.

Then shout into the valley,
    halloo the town.
Knock your head on the sea-cliff

and gather up the foam.
Run over the mountains
    under the moon.
All the lovers that you knew have
    long gone home.

PUTTING MYSELF TOGETHER

I thought that my body was muscle and bone,
and that the tough heart was a sunrise of blood.
In the cave of my mind that's what I thought.

Or my childhood thought with the whole of my body,
as though gray mind could imagine a bone
bleached in the blood of the pounding heart.

I felt that my heart was the center of thought,
each cell in the blood fed all of my body;
white in the bone, gray in the mind.

And I guessed that mind could reason the heart
or lecture the bone with a finger of thought,
or the rebel body and rebellious blood.

But always the blood flooded the mind,
and the hungry body taunted the heart
with its starlit thought and moonlit bone.

Then even the bone cried out to the blood,
Take some thought of that darkening mind
and go tell the heart to give up the body,

or give body and bone the thought of the heart,
and the blood of the mind.

THE OLD CRADLE

Yes, it is nearly morning. The sun is still darkly
winged under the horizon, but the dream of its
circumference flies along the eastern hills like some vague
flock of shadowy orioles and goldfinches. At some far signal,
lost among the amoeba and the ferns, the flesh-drugged
body is slowly moving, having just struggled out of the
mother of sleep and wandered downstairs into the kitchen
for no apparent reason, and then out to the living room for
no apparent reason either, having done nothing even
slightly practical or remotely intentional. The last ghost of
night has already slunk back into the northeastern corner of
the house, and the small geometric gnomes and figures in
the rug are just beginning to rise from the living-room floor.
The body steps remotely among them, then hesitates,
uncertain whether to disrobe toward nakedness and clean
up, as the biomorphic clock ticks on in the next room, or to
reach out somewhere for the smooth oak banister and crawl
blindly back up the wooden stairs and snuggle back on the
far side of dawn.

There in that vague light the body hesitates; it
hesitates too long, and it is all fatal, like some unwanted
glory in the clouds. That unsteady earth has kept rolling.
Even the lidded eye can see that. And now, just at the tip of
the world, there is a hard yellow glint that springs from the
forest of night right into the stunned eye and begins to
prowl in the back mirrors of the brain. At the same time,
the heart, the body's sun, murmurs above the nerves; a rusty
pump catches and lifts and falls in the throat, drains toward
the stomach and groin, and the left foot begins to tingle.

But Body, why did you stay there? You should have
left! Now it is too late, too late! There is a whole live chunk

of sunlight rainbowing through the luminous trees, and the mind, no matter how deeply it laments, knows and knows that it has abandoned its latest dream still once again among the rumpled patchwork quilts. Oh, so reluctantly. But, yes, it might as well accept this sudden gift of day, like an early phone call from a friend or the knock of an over-hearty neighbor at your door when no one, really, no one, should have been up and about.

So now—and you can't help it—the whole sun sits right on the edge of the horizon, smiling, and then, my God! it opens right off into the air like a large bright mouth talking out loud. There is no way, any longer, now, to put the sleep-warm finger of desire to your lips and say, "ssshh," or to press the heavy eyelids securely down, or even to sink down and curl up on the floor at your feet like that old cradle you fell out of years and years ago.

And oh God! the body utterly knows this. Utterly. You can't go home again. God's in his heaven now, no matter how. That much is true. You begin to yawn and, as the mouth hugely opens, the downy pillow of the cheek rises up again and the dark eyelashes come down to touch it one last time. Then you begin to lift and stretch your arms, take a step, and then another, and head for the bathroom. My goodness, the whole body is waking up; it has already gone to work.

And you still here? Well, good morning, everybody.

WATCHING ATHLETES

What is blood   but anger and love
poured in the muscle   of a full heart?

And what is bone   but a slow precision
going its way   down a long road?

And what is flesh   but the sinewy hands
pulled to a dream   of an old earth?

And what is the eye   but the asteroids
flung on the skies   by the burning stars?

And what is the tongue   but the proud mind
all exercised   with what it is?

And who am I   but all of these
trapped in itself   and grown to this.

SKY-RUNNING

What shall we ask of the exploding universe
when the whole sky
burns with one blue question
and the fields go dry in their summer crops?
Even the woodlands in their abstract hills
rise in their green enigmas . . .

I have gone down to the sky
through the blue lakes
and risen in your cool arms asking my question still.
My fingers walk
over the furrows of your brow
toward some more possible thought,
and my body runs its tunnel of leafy shade
asking why it was made.

Was it the eye of Eohippus born
that watched its ancient pasture where we ran?
Some star, or sun, or moon
rolling our empty heavens?
Or merely some leafy tassel of oats
flowering its rustling stem?
Or a kernel knit to the upper cone of our brow?

Or did some curious music,
scored for an errant wind on the long pale grass
and done to a cold and beating rain,

usher my groping hands from the old cave
and train my feet to this world?

I thought I heard you whispering,
and once when the whole blue sky was wild with clouds
a trumpet blew in my head, saying:
here is the harvest again, such as it is,
and the woodlands bare again,
and the meadows drowsy with snow,
and the horses galloping off in the springing leaves,
and the seed in the black ground,
and the whole world turning round and round and round.

ONE OF MY NEIGHBORS, TALKING

When one is troubled the heart
   makes a fist in the chest
and the mind, disturbed and silent
   in its vague unrest,

will ask us, "Why? Why?"
   Even our heavy feet
wander off to left or right,
   uncertain how to meet

that place where they were going,
   or should have gone.
Then's when the tongue mumbles,
   "Why did I let it go on?"

And the eye really doesn't focus
   on things, or remark that this
could be what it is looking for,
   or even know what it is.

And if the wrist and neck skin,
   or part of your flesh, stretches
in a most strange discomfort
   and the breath catches,

don't let it get you down. I guess
   most women and most men
have gone through all of this before,
   and will again.

DANDELION

Yellow, yellow, yellow,
weedy and earthy and juicy dandelion,
I love you, giving wings
to your dark seed, clouded with silver hair,
suspiring to your natural desecrations.

Now, in this place,
after that plush and velvet heart
gives up its character,
I feel that you are always arriving
by wandering where you will
in any wind.

Yours is a bitter root and a stout stem.
Strength by strength,
have I not gathered your deep white sockets
into my galvanized buckets
and banked them with my daily fires?

You are both a small sun
and a pale moon.
When you come
flowering through the daylight
my blood smiles in its skin;
and under any moons that I have known
those disembodied hosts of stringent mouths
still populate these bones.

Breathing that fragrance now,
something expires.

But even if you rose and turned and went
memory would keep you
rampant on its green and golden bed;
and even then, given a little time
while loneliness distills the weedy ground,
you would still be this clear white wine
sweet to my tongue,
where all these windy words and ghostly throngs
have, in your absence, come.

EARTH FARMER

Nothing that you might say can change me now.
How could I train my countenance to frown?
Or teach my eyes to say
otherwise? Or tell my body how
to shrug and rise and leave this town?
Or carelessly go away?

No, they have fixed themselves upon this place;
these are their roots; their genesis is done.
Time strikes with a hard stroke,
but its attitudes upon this face
return like singular leaves to the sun:
maple, willow, and oak.

If I put my fist in earth, bring up a hand,
and then another, then put down a seed,
all rains will heal that scar.
What overspreads the under land,
uprisen from a certain need,
is likely what we are.

A DREAM OF LOVE

Once upon a time
three brothers kept three horses
in a farmyard near a forest not far from
    a magnificent castle.
According to the old story,
one was black, one brown, and one white.
Each night one of the brothers caught his own horse
    in the early evening,
and in the glimmering darkness
he tried to ride it up a great glass hill
into that fairy kingdom.

And somewhere three beautiful horses,
with stars just under their forelocks
and hooves aglow in the moonlight,
nicker out of my childhood
and neigh in the distant meadows.
They stand at night in the pastures
with Bell and King and Beauty,
with Czar and Kate by the river
munching the grass by the timber
in the hills of northeastern Iowa,
with Blossom and Queen and Noble
wild in the harness of springtime,
tame in the woodland of summer;
with May and June, gray-dappled,
mild in their stalls in the winter,
trotting with sleighs and wagons,
straining at tugs in the snowdrifts,
farting out loud in the village,

working and sweating and sleeping;
with Roxy and Trixy and Mabel,
biting and pawing and snorting
when led to the western stallion,
ears flat on their foreheads, breeding,
their nostrils flaring, kicking,
till their hind legs set like pillars;
with Daisy and Bill and Lady
chucking for oats in the morning,
chortling for hay in the evening,
and at county fairs with sulkies
racing with silver jockeys
and galloping over the hillsides.

My hands still fiddle with those bridles still,
the steel bits sliding over the white shining teeth,
past the dark elastic lips and pink tongues
swallowing into their soft throats.
I pull the reins taut; my arms tighten on their sleek
    muscles,
and again the polished hooves go clattering
out of the moonlit barnyard and on to the glass hill
where the breathless lady waits with her gossamer
    gowns and pale lips, chill as the night,
for the breath of her one true lover.

Daisy and Lady and Beauty,
we curry your hair in the morning,
your manes in the morning combing,
braiding your tails in the morning,
your velvet nostrils rubbing,
your rumps all silken, slapping;
on your barrel backs still climbing

I bury my face in your manes.
I snuggle my crotch on your withers,
my legs on your rib-flanks wrapping
to touch my feet to your belly.
And we walk and trot and gallop
out of the barns to the roadway
and up the road to the mailbox
and over the hills to the neighbors,
then back again to the barnyard
where I clean your stalls of manure
and bed you down for the evening
in bundles of golden straw.

Black Beauty, I think, is still whinnying
    in the orchards and weeping by waterfalls.
Postilions, coaches and schooners are running wild
    in their old tracks.
Flicka has tossed her tail up again west of Cheyenne
    and is headed into the mountains.
Smoky the Cowhorse is languishing in his harness,
trying to make that shriveled heart grow back again
    to full size.
The Red Pony and spotted horses are asleep in the
    bookshelves,
and Rosa Bonheur has scribbled magnificent horses
    all over the one-room schoolhouse wall.

Horses are standing by roadways,
charging over the sagebrush
in their oiled and studded saddles;
they are swimming the swollen rivers
through Wyoming, leaping and bucking
and plunging in dust storms of cattle;

Old Paint is off to Montana,
walking the tourists in mountains
and standing by livery stables
and threshing grain on the prairies.

And somewhere in the local theaters of Spring Grove,
    Minnesota, and Decorah, Iowa,
legions of horses are rising and leaping out of
    the wild Atlantic
onto the Brittany beaches.
Their seaweed manes are rising and falling,
    their hooves
rising and falling, the wind-driven grass rising
and falling over the dunes,
and the dark French rustlers with their stiff
    black hats
are throwing silver lariats everywhere
    out of the hills.

And the Good Men are riding their horses,
and the Bad Men riding their horses,
the stagecoach is whipping its horses,
and the Indians are riding their horses,
and the Tartars are riding their horses,
and Genghis Khan and the Chinese
emperors riding their horses.
And horses are guarding the palace,
and Lawrence is riding his horses
with all his Arabians running
to the muffled drums of the sand.

And the great blue horses of Franz Marc
stand in Bavaria near Benedicktbüren with their strict
    geometric rumps,

and Dutch horses wait near courtyards fat as burghers.
By the hay wains set by streams, horses are no more
    than a mound or a lamp post.
And where is that young blue Spanish boy with his
    elegant mare?
Are they dreaming of blankets of flowers
falling over the pastel horses charging through
    steeplechases out of the suburbs of Paris?
Or the cavalry milling by Moscow, the horses like
    dreary plains?
Or horses like trumpets and bugles falling,
    bloodstained, out of the sky?

There are princes arriving on chargers
and departing, forever and ever,
where the farm boys sleep with their horses,
and horses hidden in thickets
while the cavalry passes on horses,
and horses pressed against boulders
while the posse passes on horses,
and horses stilled in the hemlocks
while the murderers spur at their horses,
and the hunters go by on their horses
past rivers and castles and mountains.

And still the corporal is rearing upon his stallion in
    the Louvre,
and the generals sit stiffly astride their bronze studs
in all the public squares of Europe,
and Xanthus sulks with Achilles,
and Pegasus rides from the sea foam,
Al Borak carries Mohammed,
Bucephalus, Alexander,
and Sleipnir trots with Odin

out of the fjords to the ocean;
then out of the long processional friezes
where the marble horses twist and prance for the proud
    cities
Apollo rides straight up like thunder into the skies.

And the horses are fled in the passes
with the horn of Roland winding
and Charlemagne riding his horses
and Joan of Arc at the crossroads
and the highwaymen riding their horses.
Brazilian horses are running,
and the listener sits in the moonlight,
alone on his horse in the moonlight,
with his horse in a dream forever.
Eohippus sleeps in the lavas;
and the Hittites' horses are running;
Mesohippus sleeps in the lavas;
the Persian horses are running.
In the steppes the horses are plunging
with stars just under their forelocks;
they are galloping over the tundra;
they are leaping from mountain to mountain
with hooves aglow in the moonlight.
They have harnessed the waves of the ocean.
They are riding up over our beaches.
They are running wild in our cities.
I love you! I love you!

And then the brown horse and the black horse and the
    white horse
leaped so high in the moonlight that when they came
    back down
there was only a dappled one,

and he floated up out of the back pastures over
   the hills of northeastern Iowa.
And when he came to your garden
where you sat in a blue dress on a pallet on the lawn
his hooves rang like polished bells,
and he knelt on his silken hocks and knees by your side,
laid his slender head gently upon your lap,
looked up at your face with his marble eye,
then folded the silver membrane of his eyelid down,
and slept,
scarcely hearing the apocalypse
galloping away in the shadows.

A SNOWFALL

Most ordinary in our flesh,
more sacred in ourselves,
we stride in the high snows
where the cool moon fell.

Words are a light, also,
with which we find
lowlands of blue waters.
Sun shines. Sun shines.

Winter is a pure summer
frozen in dark boughs;
green leaf, warm stone and waters
remember their weather now.

Snowfalls of all good-nights
angle into the trees;
we flash by, we flash by,
a legend in that dream.

All earth puts out my hand,
and all earth, yours.
Both warm and cold they hold
to the swift rise of years.

Snow in New England hills
and dark ponds under the snow—
though roots sleep in chilled waters,
they know. They know.

GETTING READY TO REALLY LEAVE

Then, gathering in the dusk,
comes the strange long possibility of loneliness.
Some simple rolling tune invades the dark,
routing all that nostalgic poise
of half shadows.
He stands, alone in an open room,
listening.

A moth beats at the rusted back-door screen;
a stray car hums in another street.
Old songs, old songs:
someone is going; someone is going away . . .
And then that tune, like a sentimental favorite
waltzing mindlessly around the years of young nights
and floating over the glamorous local stages
of county fairs,
trembles once more,
follows an echo further down the street,
falters, fades in again,
and is gone.

We swing for an utter moment upon that hinge—
hello, Somebody—
hover, ever so briefly upon that porch,
impersonal as the summer air,
and move on out
into the perfect silence of the town.

III

TRYING IT ALL OUT

Earth
is a home of credibilities.
I dance
within her old gyrations like a snail.
How shall I ever leave this shell of stone?

Air
is an intricate bell.
All possibility
rises and shines in her transparencies:
that huge blue flower.
How shall I keep my tenement in space?

Fire
is the cooled stone of private desperations.
It burns
in all the old geologies of death.
How shall I ever warm this house of ash?

Water
is any bird flying, a wind, a wave.
Astonishment upon astonishment
washes our muscularities:
wings, jewels, and ponds.
Man is of water made; in earth and body
that is our buoyant home.

LIBERTYVILLE

(*for Adlai*)

The state tree, bird and flower of Illinois are the oak,
cardinal and violet

There is a fountain in a wood
and by the fountain a green oak,
and in the oak a cardinal,
and near the oak's abiding root
a leaf and flower of violet.
And if the elder oak be green,
the redbird's whistle clear in tone
and the low violet sweet in bloom,
that's half a rainbow, but the rest
        depends on us.

There is a river in that wood
of sky-blue water, and a disk
of midnight sun and midday moon;
if any traveler, looking out
from the deep shadow of his mind,
can tell what banks to lie upon
and drink beyond confusion,
        that's half a rainbow.

There is a flower at the edge
of the blue water. In the oak
the sun and moon have built a nest;
and in that nest, you may have heard,
there is a bird, there is a bird.

And in his beak there is a leaf.
Now in the morning of a death
I dream of Noah, riding high
upon some possibility
toward Africa and Everest.
But that's a rainbow. And the tale
is fragmentary. Still, the rest
      depends . . .

WALDEN

When I first went to Walden Pond
alone in the afternoon of the last day of summer
in the centennial of his death
the woods rang with sparrows, squirrels and crows.
Turning around the rockpile of Thoreau's hut
I discovered, also, that I had been born
in the centennial of his birth.
There in the lifted day, Icarian bird,
I circled the dark edge of an ancient dream
and started down to the water.

And the very first person I met upon my path
was a tall young Negro.
He stood easily by the woodsy pond
with his white girl friend,
casually linking their hands by a leaning birch.
Its leaves quivered in a light breeze
wakening over the dark waters,
and under the random clouds in that deep sky
we smiled, and I went on.

And the very next person I met upon that path
was a brown man from India
lounging in mottled pebbles and blond sand
with a college sweatshirt hung on his shoulders.
Into that lake he dipped his golden hands;
he turned his palms in the common water
and lifted them, all spangled,
in the mystical geometry of light.
Drops fell in a chain
and linked their circular furrows on the pond.

A frog plunked from the bank;
an autumn leaf swung down.
A blue jay screamed;
we smiled, and I went on.

And further along the brightly shadowed woods
the very next person I met upon that path
was a wild white man
running and leaping through the brush,
mumbling some half-hummed song as he ran.
His jacket was flung open;
his face shone with light;
and a rumpled paisley muffler of rainbowing colors
trailed from his torn pocket
and waved
in floating arcs among the aisles of trees,
frightening the song sparrows into sudden answers
as he fled on.

And then, at a further turn, I met myself.
I smiled and stepped to the tall and weedy shades
at the small bay on the western edge,
stripped to my native self
on brackish ground and shining sand
and, walking into the sun from tufted sedge
past polliwogs, mud flats and water spiders,
I strode those slippery shoals to the clear blue
and dove in calm delight
to thrash my limbs and throw my pale white arms
around those springing waters,

Seeing the afternoon break from the woods
I heard the long dark tale of history flashing down

and rose in a clear dream.
Simply jeweled with all that pond
I put my homely raiment on
and rode the luminous hum of the blue-gray twilight
through Concord, all the way back
to my Amherst American home.

A SMALL RANT IN FAVOR OF CIVILIZATION

Imagine some denials, if you will:
Chartres and the Taj Mahal and the Parthenon
unquarried in some geologic hill
with sheep and shepherds stumbling on the stone,

or Michelangelo a tool of war;
Dante merely a lover, Ghibelline;
Bach a whistle carver, nothing more;
Beethoven herding donkeys by the Rhine;

or the sacred texts but hieroglyphs in sand
and only natural beauty near at hand.

THINKING OF MELVILLE IN HIS
THIRTEENTH LAND-LOCKED YEAR
AT ARROWHEAD

(after a dark starry night spent singing his phrases
from the 23rd chapter of *Moby Dick*)

Deep memories yield no epitaphs.
This six-inch chapter is a stoneless grave,
a storm-tossed ship
miserably driving along the leeward land
past safety, comfort, friends—
all that is kind to our mortalities.

One touch of land,
though it but graze the keel
would make her shudder through and through,
seeking the lashed sea's landlessness again.
The wildest winds conspire
to cast us on that treacherous, slavish shore.

Know ye, for refuge,
forlornly rushing into peril,
all deep and earnest thinking
is but the intrepid effort of the soul to keep
the open independence of her sea.

Shoreless, indefinite as God,
it is better to perish in that howling infinite.
Worm-like, then,
oh! who would craven crawl to land!

Melville, Melville, Melville,
we know thee now.
Take heart, take heart.
Up from the spray of thy ocean-perishing,
straight up,
leaps thy apotheosis:
the great gray shroud of the sea.

WINDFLOWER SONGS: FOR HARVEY SWADOS

He loved the olives of Southern France and the maples
here, Brooklyn Heights and the Village and Washington Mews,
the Berkshires and Chesterfield Gorge, his flute and the piano
and harp, Mozart and Beethoven and Mahler, Stendhal and
the memoirs of Herzen, anemones, cardinals, airedale dogs,
yes, and the color blue.

—Bette Swados

The olive and the maple stand,
a southern slope, a northern land,
and take by local presence there
a range of color from the air.

For leaf, one makes a duller green:
the maple brighter, shade and sheen.
One maintains it to the end;
the other flames and comes again.

For sky, one asks a softer blue,
Mediterranean in its hue;
the other likes it sharp and bold:
blue that blazes, blue that's cold.

And both are harps that in them tell
insects and parasites, as well;
the old dove from the olive calls,
from maple, whistling cardinals.

For structure, one is twisted, spread;
the other towers overhead.
One, sun and shadow interlaid,
the other, deep in summer shade.

One likes the Berkshires for a stance;
the other, all of Southern France.
They bless our villages and prove
as graceful in a country grove.

Take your Stendhal and your dog;
sit down against a maple log,
and page through one provincial town
while Julian brings the olives down.

Then read by shovel, pick and hoe,
by shrill assemblies, row by row,
a raging fist of words. Then shout.
And love? It simply knocked him out.

The maple's juice is sugar-sweet,
the olive bitter. When we eat,
as when we talk, the mind is stung
by such a balance on the tongue.

Carve maple, olive, flute by flute,
they keep the hardness of their root,
and hold such grains before our eyes
as took an age to compromise.

That tough discretion grows and clear
the humors of a hundred years.
God, bring an olive from the South
and hard rock maple from the North.

No matter where they stood, or are,
their nature is their metaphor:
a celebration, known at last
by overflowing, standing fast.

TALKING OUT LOUD TO SOMEONE
I ONCE TALKED TO

("Young poetry is the breath of parted lips."—R.F.)

The declination of the leaves
is not, alone, decline;
they also grow.
Not in themselves, transported,
but in the long luxurious flow
of root to wing
until they rise again
upon another limb,
exclaiming, "Here I am!"

The eye is keener for its age,
as well as less.
The fingers, yes,
a bit more dull
but lined and beautiful.
The ear more slack, and yet the note it hears
more simply music,
collaborating with the tongue
for fifty years since they were young.

I'm with you, Robert, in your brief surmise
discovered seemingly at play,
almost of silence made,
knowing that what you say
parted your lips at eighty, being wise.

DOWN UNDER OUR DAYS

The little animals walk in the night woods. Grass listens on the ground and the leaves in their tall trees. Something is sitting up on its hind paws; jet eyes peer around in the darkness; pointed ears stiffen under the stars. Something moves and sweeps along the ground. Hearts in their furry breasts palpitate, and thin tails flick, electric with darkness. They quiver delicately; they turn; even among their own kind something is unfriendly. Somewhere, nearby, another animal is getting ready to pounce while natural unlovely warfare walks in the night woods. Now they are all alive with fear. They start in their own shrouds. I see them darting into strange holes, hanging on tenuous limbs, and running over the green leaves. They are hiding in a little shrub of weeds, their paws half lifted, shivering.

       Still from the dreamy edges I hear them scuffling in the leaves under my window. I hear their little throbs of delight; they break in brief amusement through the grass. They stand up with skittery eyes, peering upon the palaces of men. I hear the little animals of night. Oh, keep my sleeping eyes alive to love, my skin all prickly with affection. Here in the dream-swept velvet whispering nights we sleep the troubling darkness of our days.

A HIROSHIMA LULLABY*

Sadako, you have gone
beyond the fire's fear;
we follow where you walk
upon that magic hill.

The Hiroshima birds
come back across the sea
into the city square.
Sleep now, Sadako, sleep.

Now on the darkest nights
the shadows on the waves
lift from your fallen eyes
upon a cloud of cranes.

They march across the sky,
a thousand in a line
to keep their watch upon
the children in their dreams.

Sadako, here's a star
to cradle in your hand

* For Sadako Sasaki, dead of leukemia in October, 1955, at the age of
twelve. A few months before her death she tried to fold 1,000 paper cranes
which, according to Japanese legend, would protect her health. She had
reached 964 when she died. Her childhood classmates completed the magic
thousand and raised money for her statue, holding a golden crane, in the
Peace Park in Hiroshima.

and fly around the sun
and nest upon the moon.

Sadako, paper girl,
ride on your thousand wings
and cry your gentle prayer.
We fold your paper cranes.

THE LOTUS FLOWER

(In 1840, the year of his marriage to Clara, Robert Schumann wrote
138 songs, of which "The Lotus Flower" is one.)

Now it is one hundred and thirty-six years later.
For almost a month now,
from the 14th of June to the 4th of July,
I have been trying to sing "The Lotus Flower" by
   Schumann
to an English text adapted from Heinrich Heine.
The days burn toward the sun;
the flower turns toward the moon.

Through oaks and maples at my eastern windows
clear radiance flows down upon my house.
This sun, at its generous distance,
marries the elements and warms me.
Last night
I even thought I saw it smiling in the full face
   of the moon.
I, too, might blossom there,
as I think I almost do
in this song, in this room, in these strings,
under the arch of these boughs,

but

thirty-one years ago
I stood in my infantry soldier's uniform
puzzling out the elaborate German Gothic lettering
of some lines from Heinrich Heine—
"Let not disgusting worms consume my body;
give me the clear bright flame"—

done on parchment in an oaken frame
over the concrete arch
of the door to the crematorium
at Buchenwald, nach Weimar,
where three brick ovens
fed their red hearts to the sun.

My hands, in the six-four time, keep faltering
heavily over the black and white keys
and I hear my voice saying, "The lotus flower
lies drooping
under the sun's warm light,"
over those huge repeated modulating chords.

I sit in the mottled sunlight of my home
more than four thousand miles away,
alone in another hemisphere.
As the chords change
my foot lifts and falls on the left steel pedal,
dampening the discords.

Again my hands pause; my foot wanders, waits.
So as not to stumble,
I lift it carefully over the concrete doorsill.
My voice begins to fail. The sun
glows on the low barracks. Through the square door
the light shifts
in the green leaves and sifts
over our white faces
like ashes.

I close the piano; I put my book away
and head for the outside door,
sunlit and gray.

A STONE FOR A MAKER

(Rolfe Humphries, 1894–1969)

Brought to this old translation of ourselves,
    imagining truth to the source,
we lie in a mask of memory under the quick
    eyelids of our world.
                    I woke, he almost said,
                    to the thought of music.
A playful light, transparent, folds and lifts,
    turns in a shadow, smiles
in crafty undulations, then gathers in
    word upon phrase on line.
                    Three sirens sat in the barley,
                    fluting upon a straw.
Once, in a greener country, David went
    humming through hedge and farm,
ragged among the brambles. He taught his tongue
    the grace of a strong harp;
                    Even the daylight, itself,
                    practiced upon his fingers.
he made it shake the heavy weeds with love
    and riffle the village streams,
while flocks of flittering sparrows broke the clumps
    of thistles into a sweet
                    (How sweet that music was,
                    the song that silences)
suspended audience. Listen to the measure
    vibrating the very airs
of the strung throat of the hoarse singer still
    twanging among the heralds.

Beating a stick on a stump
is almost enough for a drum.
Hunger, he sang, and hollow absence flung
over the rocky halls,
and soiled mantles, drifting upon the wind,
and love, a broken psalm.
It's what we mend that makes
us menders of anything.
And mercy, whoever he is, he cried for him,
that white and tardy fool
running the seas and hills. How shall we keep
justice snug in our rooms?
There are many answers, too.
Try one, he said, on me.
Or green armor on green ground? Or the cunning
harp in broken hands?
Or bend the words to the song, making them do
what the poem understands?
Everything comprehends
itself in becoming itself.
So rags for the body, sing, and a cup of beer,
and sing the ruddy fire,
and a few companions to pluck away the nights
from the battering bell of time.
And if time does not ring
hc'll clap it to, again.
Then let the vasty spirits of the cliffs
rage on the vales and coves
and run the greenest valley underground,
loving the dumb stones.

UPON HEARING HIS HIGH SWEET TENOR AGAIN

John McCormack, you are riding again the air
in Italian arias and Irish chants
   like an old boyish want.

My father saved your records, played your songs
for twenty-one years from nineteen-eight and on
   clear into the Depression.

Then I cut the wooden needles when the steel
gave out on the Victrola. And I watched
   your voice in static etched

go faintly skipping and flying in our home,
delicate, robust and pure. Throat and tongue
   caressed each note and sang

so that a boy, all ignorant of music,
voice or life itself, could steal from the air
   such intimations there

that though we labored round an endless wheel
and rolled with it, resounding day to day
   vibrating in an old groove,

still neither death nor poverty nor crime
can ever from his ear or eye remove
   such resonance, such love.

WITH JOHN MATHISON IN WYOMING

He was our Johnson and our Boswell, too,
making our praise and observations true.
Sunlight was sunlight, and a shade a shade,
unless a metaphor for wit were made;
then fancy would enliven everything,
fools would be local gods, and monotones would sing.

I see him now, half poised upon a word,
amused before the syllables were heard
with what he sensed before he said it out,
and what he felt before he spoke it out:
the pleasures of intelligence, unstressed,
held back one moment, wisely, and then well expressed.

I've seen him lean in springtime on a hoe
meaning to let some thing or other grow,
and in high summer lean upon his lawn,
and then upon a rake till autumn's gone,
and lean upon a spade in winter snow,
letting such labors come, easily letting them go.

For jacket, any tweed, though patched, would do,
and for formality, striped navy blue,
two-three dark ties, knotted, a bit askew.
The modish styles were not his cry and hue.
And a Plymouth fordor, modest in decor,
got him wherever we got, in time, or just before.

If one eye drew him inward into thought,
the other hovered outward till it caught
the rhythm of that moment in his mind

and balanced there, somehow, with human kind.
The one knit eyebrow hid its point within;
the other rose in triumph, arched above his grin.

and when perplexity undid us all
in talk too muddily political,
he'd wrap his legs around a table leg,
and then unwrap them on another leg
and rear back, hanging on an epithet
that left the quarreling parties chuckling in his debt.

He was High-Plains Augustan, born too late
to do a Cromwell in, or save a state;
with him the clergy, governor, or dude
too richly gowned came off a bit more nude.
Catholic in his tastes, his humors ran
at length when Lutheran, or local Anglican.

At lectures he was frequently amused
by what the speaker thought his mind perused,
and at the theater suddenly might roar
at what the besieged director let indoor,
and at a student concert, out of dread,
half turn and duck beneath the coda with his head.

Once, when a conference room was over-full
with pious platitudes and thoughtless wool,
and the ruffled chairman sought for any out,
casting his small beseeching eyes about,
even that meeting might have been worth saving
if John had only muttered what his mind was raving.

He was no cowboy, but he did ride herd
on any infelicity of word

and quote a misquotation like a gun
aimed at its error; and when that was done
he'd blow the whole thing into something bigger,
cock the blessed thing, and pull the unerring trigger.

We've seen him take a flight of purple prose,
dangle it sagely under moustache and nose,
then try it out, most solemnly and wise,
like some amazing bird of paradise,
then pluck the pompous feathers from its squawk
done in with a small bag of unpretentious talk.

And sometimes, when his mind outran the class
and he paused, hopefully, for lad or lass
to phrase some question he had left behind,
in passing, in a previous state of mind,
his lips danced half the distance to their tongues
to tease articulation up and outward from their lungs.

Somehow, in memory, I can't suppress
a smile, thinking of John. For he could dress
a Bronte in the lineaments of place
and do up Fielding in a squire's face,
or hold a sentimental trip in hand
like a fat Christmas pie, or a curate's contraband.

I'd like to call him up and say that some
few friends are coming over, can you come,
and meet him at the door and ask him in,
offer a chair, crackers & cheese, some gin,
then settle back, with mock sobriety,
and let the whole long evening saunter slowly by,

remarking this or that, or thinking of
friends and our weather, politics and love.
Some games are done for keeps, and some for chance,
but somewhere in this breezy nonchalance
the memory stumbles, just in getting on
word by word by word, out there without you, John.

UPON LEAVING A FOLK STORY UNFINISHED

Suddenly, halfway through an old tale
he stopped in the deep wood and turned pale,
and each loud confident broad word
could be scarcely heard.
It was as though some vague and threatening rumor
had snagged and tripped his humor.
The swaggering body in its brave laugh
went crippled, cut in half,
and the starry faces of his world were caught and thrown
from their high blue attitudes down
into the black premises of earth, unknown,
and heaved up, stone by stone.

ARCANUM

Found in the high arcanum of her sleep,
   my sister death
   walks with a severe breath
among the parlors that her families keep.

Where she is most at home and always most
   generous and kind,
   we now find
her house inhabited by a most ungenerous host.

Something far less than kind, far less than good,
   invades her daily now,
   having somehow
laid down its dark destroyer in her blood.

And there it mocks her will, muscle and nerves,
   consuming away
   the daily bread of her day,
a stranger company than she deserves.

Religion, medicine, philosophy, and care
   in turn arouse
   themselves about her house.
This is not mercy or justice; this is not fair.

Some are obliged by fate. And there are some
   who come by chance
   on evil in the merest glance
and are, thereby, exiled out of house and home.

But I will not clasp this stranger to my breast
   and call it good,
   or be told that I should.
Good labor well deserves a better rest.

Meanwhile, this is the present fate we have.
   Therefore, while I still live
   I will receive and give
all that I can, all the way to the grave.

A LITTLE DAY-MUSIC
FOR MY DEPARTED SISTER

Corrine, wake up!   the dog's at the door,
truck in the yard,   dust on the floor,
flies on the screen;   the swinging clock
is the day's chores   and the heart's knock.

That deep sigh   for all that has been
is only a whisper   of an old pain
that is dying away   in memory, green
as a fair life   and a good name.

The blue skies   are tilled and plowed,
filled up with sun,   pulled down with cloud.
Friends and neighbors,   fancy and plain,
do what you know,   see what you've seen.

Nothing the earth   can yield to us
is more than your shovel   uplifting a rose,
more than your kitchen   flooded with light,
bright in the morning,   dark in the night.

Corrine, wake up!   All we have known
of wheat kernels   and heart stones
is little beside   the proud blood
that carried your head   in our neighborhood.

The graveled roads   run up and down;
friends still walk   in Decorah, Waukon;
and the days rise,   brown white black green
among your heartiest   loves, Corrine.

Corrine, wake up!   and greet the morn.
Your rose by the kitchen   is fragrant, the thorn
is polished with dew   and the sweet alarm
of the sun invading   the underground.

Now even the root   of death is calm,
and the far night   and northwest storm.
And we are abroad   in earth and flame
to call from the air   once more, your name.

Corrine, wake up!   dogs at the door,
trucks in the yard,   dust on the floor.
Too much to do   before you lie down,
or put on your dress   and ride into town.

Too much to think of,   rain, wind, and sun,
the house untidy,   the days undone
night after night   and dawn after dawn.
God only knows   where you might have gone.

LISTENING

Someone is sleeping a thousand miles from here
   who will not be sleeping long.
Each of us must awaken to learn to sleep;
   to be weak one must be strong.

Someone is breathing a thousand miles from here
   who will breathe but a few days more;
in a little while, friends will be only strangers
   passing along her door.

Someone is listening a thousand miles from here
   for what eardrums cannot find;
what she is hearing only one mind can know,
   and that not long in mind.

Someone is waking a thousand miles from here
   to familiar women and men.
But simply to waken, alive, was a kind of grace
   we assumed, again and again.

Now someone is thinking, someone thinks, I know,
   and it shames me because it seems
unspeakable, final and clear, and we are vague
   as a sleepwalking riddle of dreams

that answer to breath and sound and thought, and yes
   to sleep that is over and done
and flesh that loved, was loved, and is falling under
   a chaste and chiseled stone.

HOLDING THEM STILL

When we are up and about, all sleep seems
a starlit silence, as though the soul might well
forget a third of its days, breathy with dreams.

Yet sometimes, in early autumn, we get
all along the western horizon for an hour
just after the sun has set,

especially when country and town
have been without any rain for a little while,
the graces of earth in a blue crown

entirely luminous and clear.
Yes, in such a tremulous hour we get
the sense of far things being near.

Why, we can see for miles everywhere.
There is nothing that seems either too far away
or yet too near. Look there!

at that tree way off, and this easily seen
burr oak tree that is standing beside us here—
both the same posture of darkening green.

And even though one is larger and nearer
it would not seem right for anyone to claim
that either is sharper or clearer.

Perhaps such prefigurations can trail
our winking and blinking on retina and nerve,
like faith upon hope until we fail

and our bodies merely serve
as an ancient school of memory; earth and sky
fade in their spaces as into a curve

of sparkling darkness. Try
as we may we cannot, simply cannot, hold them still.
They grace, moment by moment, the severe eye,

outdistancing ourselves. They darken our will.
See! they are going: these hands, this tree there,
our road, those upland fields, that further hill,

while sun and sky, the parasitical green,
subside in muffled shadows, sheen on sheen,
and glow in the dust and dew, unseen,

like Karen, Clara Elizabeth, and Corrine.

DAILINESS

Free-falling, free-floating,
each nameless day comes down
upon its crumpled canopy of cloud.

The long strings of the sun
pull from the sky
dray horse and chariot.

The iron wheels spin
behind the leather tugs and jeweled bridle.
Then we in our flowing robes

come drifting downward. Down we come
in all our houses.
Doors open. We walk among our homes.

REINCARNATION

I would come back to you as a tall green willow;
but if not a tree, let me rise up as a hawk;
and if not a bird, then the magical number seven;
and if not a number, shy and wise in a fox;
and if not an animal made, then blue, sky-blue;
and if not a color, I'll be a wild wild rose.

Five petals circle the heart of the wild wild rose;
a garland of leaves encircles the limb of a willow;
sunlight, clouds, and a white moon circle the blue;
circling upon his circles, floats the hawk;
circling his den, unseen, now enters the fox;
and sisters, muses, and gods all circle in seven.

And what two shapes are blessing the number seven?
And what two colors blush to the wild wild rose?
And what two barnyard animals envy the fox?
And pray, what rises only to fall in the willow?
What is the prism of black in the breast of a hawk?
And why is the distant light in the legend blue?

Blood, in its royal courtship, worships blue.
Square and triangle marry together in seven.
Rainbow sleeps like a wishbone hung in the hawk.
Rose-White and Rose-Red curtsy the wild wild rose.
Each branch goes up to bow in the supple willow.
And dog and cat would run and leap like a fox.

I have slept in winter fur of an old trapped fox
and fallen asleep in a summer eyelid of blue

and gathered my face to the autumn leaves of willow.
I have risen at seven and fallen asleep at seven
and spied on the dawn of spring by the wild wild rose
while earth shook night and day from the eye of a hawk.

So I would return, like love, to the loop of the hawk;
like love, to the family cave of the secret fox;
like love, the glory of God, to the wild wild rose;
like love, fallen down on its knees in a wimple
    of blue;
like one two love, three four love, five six seven;
like love, our forefather, home to an ancient willow.

If you sing me the hawk, he is lying up there in
    the blue;
if you riddle me seven divines, then one is a fox,
one sleeps by the willow and another dreams
    of the rose.

BLOOD SONG

Earth, be intimate with blood.
  Breath, be gently warm.
Body, leap up with this heart.
  Heart, recall the mind.
And mind, be veined as any earth
  and keeper of the air,
embracing water like the sun
  to raise my body here.
I would give all my words away
  to man, woman and child,
for earth and water, fire and air,
  body, heart and mind.

SINGING IN LATE SUMMER

Singing at the piano, in late summer,
a Nordic folksong, *Den Store Hvide Flok,*
by the two windows
in the northwest corner of our living room
with one blue with late light over the western hills
and the other wide on the deep thicket of evening,
here in my home in western Massachusetts,

and my father ten years dead
and my mother eighty years old a thousand miles away
and slowly growing older,
and my eight brothers and sisters, blood of my heart,
scattered dead and alive over the face of the earth,
and my wife absent a while from these rooms she made,
and my children lately gone,

I feel the hollows under the shadowy woods
moistly expand and move,
gathering the strange authority of darkness
and breathing and seeping and creeping under the sills
until the flipping pages of my mind
wave like ghosts in the windowpane
and turn my booming song of the Great White Host
back to that black and tremulous silence
from which, I suppose, it came.

POSTSCRIPT

I hear the cry, "Be natural!" and then I walk out and examine rocks, leaves, grass, birds, animals, people, the flow of wind and fire and water. They all cry out, "Form!" Without it all reproductive things die out. The absence of form is unnatural . . . The history of poetry in English tells us, surely, that there are many roads which, if traveled well, lead to good poems. That pantheon is polytheistic; its citizens are polyglot . . . Let prosody follow, not lead. Let the spider spin and the fox breed. Then follow, follow, follow. The priorities of creation, as we can discern them, are primarily inductive. We have to take the Original Secret on faith. Our natural excitement starts from the other end, trailing emotion and wonder as it comes . . .

There are ways of training one's sensibility which parallel, say, the physical training of an athlete, or the occupational conditioning for various professions. I believe in a kind of inspiration, but it comes most often to those who work at it . . . Most good poems are unbalanced in favor of the art of their own ideas. They do not want to be neutral, nor does the poet behind them . . . It is both popular and easy to forsake art in favor of the propaganda of the "right" idea . . . The emotion of a poem is meant to distinguish and perpetuate the ephemera of our lives . . .

For a writer, his past is his good luck, no matter what luck it has been . . . No writer has come to terms with himself until he can largely see what he locally knows and provincially commands; then he can make the subject knowingly happen . . . Art depends upon life. Any life—if we look at the lives and backgrounds of artists we admire— it seems, will do. The difference is how you think with whatever you think with. Any localist has a world at hand . . .

Place is important to me. I like to have a sense of being rooted wherever I am, and many of my metaphors and the landscapes with which I think come from a firm sense of place . . . I feel a strong acceptance of the cyclic process. Dismay and grief, yes; cynicism and despair, no. The natural world teaches us this . . . The significant texture of our lives is made up out of a small number of extraordinary responses to a huge number of ordinary experiences . . . The ways in which the world regenerates itself are astonishing beyond belief. Part of the obligation of poetry is to look at it and imagine at least a little of what it is . . .

I want to use formal and colloquial language, together: a language of the street and the home, of the barn and the house. I want to yoke the ordinary speech and idiom of my youth to rhetoric and elegance. I want to write American poems without denying my English or my Norwegian-American heritage . . . Daily speech, itself, is closer to the speaking voice than almost any poem, and it is usually undistinguished . . . In a journal, it is a temptation to demystify experience without finding the crucial memorable phrase . . .

Everyone should hear a few poems said in the absolute darkness. That forces one to really hear the language. It is easy to tell a good poem in the darkness . . . I could spontaneously sing a whole poetry reading, making it up, such as it was, as I went along. Good readers understand this inclination . . . To the poet, all language is a kind of music. And the line? It is like a bell. It needs to be rung, but it need not be rung regularly; an occasional sounding will often do, and do well.

—Joseph Langland